MIDNIGHT
SNACKS

MIDNIGHT SNACKS

THE COOKBOOK THAT GLOWS IN THE DARK

Carol Schneider and Andrew Schneider

Clarkson Potter/Publishers New York

Published by Clarkson N. Potter, Inc., 201 East 50th Street, New York, New York 10022. Member of the Crown Publishing Group.

Random House, Inc. New York, Toronto, London, Sydney, Auckland.

Clarkson N. Potter, POTTER, and colophon are trademarks of Clarkson N. Potter, Inc.

Manufactured in the U.S.A.

Design by Renato Stanisic

Library of Congress Cataloging-in-Publication Data
Schneider, Carol E.
   Midnight snacks : the cookbook that glows in the dark / by Carol Schneider and Andrew Schneider.
   1. Snack foods. 2, Quick and easy cookery. I. Schneider, Andrew. II. Title.
TX740.S3255   1994
   641.5'3--dc20   94-21968
                           CIP
ISBN 0-517-70029-8

10   9   8   7   6   5   4

CONTENTS

INTRODUCTION

Of all the times of day for indulging the urge to snack, midnight is clearly the hour of preference. It's the time when appetites are truly sharpened, when even adults who have outgrown the child's need for constant fuel discover special cravings. And oh, the pleasure of it! The silent house, the beckoning refrigerator, the absence of anyone who might raise an eyebrow or remind you to put away the meat loaf...

The midnight snack has a long and venerable history, but its partisans must have been too sleepy to record it; we have not yet found a reference to it in any book of food lore or history. On our own, we've been able to trace it back to the court of Louis XIV, when sweet green peas were introduced in France. They became such a rage that courtiers at Versailles had plates of peas delivered to their rooms to nibble on before going to bed. After that, the trail disappears and doesn't pick up again until Dagwood Bumstead and his famous sandwiches. But we'll keep looking.

What does seem clear is that midnight snacking is a universal practice. Snackers come in all shapes and sizes, ages and occupations. They are children, they are students, they are lovers, they are insomniacs, they are solitary people in search of some comfort food, they are busy executives fueling themselves to get through the homework in their briefcases, they are members of a family sneaking into the darkened kitchen at various times of night. We have written this book for all of them, and as mother and son we probably represent virtually every constituency.

A WORD FROM THE MOTHER

My own history with midnight snacks reaches deep into my past. As a child, my favorite moment to strike was after my parents had a dinner party. I devised the Refrigerator Smorgasbord, pulling up a chair to the open fridge and sticking a finger into anything that looked inviting. Adulthood, with its tiresome awareness of electrical bills and food spoilage, has forced me to abandon my open-door policy—which my mother was never crazy about, anyway—in favor of a modified version where I actually put things on a plate.

Having nourished three sons through the teenage years, I consider myself an expert on the subject of snacks, midnight or otherwise. I never fail to leave the supermarket without casting an embarrassed glance over my shoulder (can I pretend I'm buying for a Boy Scout troop? an orphanage? the Visigoths?). On one memorable occasion, I purchased fourteen packages of a favorite frozen pasta dinner which was on sale that week, only to discover, five days later, that the freezer bore no trace of it. "There's no food in the house!" is a common complaint. And it's no wonder, when all the leftover spaghetti and half a banana cream pie are a trifle eaten after school, and when something described by the manufacturer as a frozen "dinner" is consumed in pairs several hours after a perfectly normal-size meal has been served.

Andrew, oldest of my three sons and my cooking partner for this book, still has a youthful lack of inhibition, as I did when I sat before the open fridge. One of his favorite ploys is to stick his hand into this week's cereal-of-choice and grab a handful. He does this in spite of his brothers' howls that having his dirty mitt in the Honey Nut Cheerios makes it considerably less appetizing for anyone else. And perhaps that's the point: Andrew has been known to squirrel away a particularly appealing box of cookies or cereal on a shelf with, say, the laundry detergent or the light bulbs, just to cut down on the chances of anyone else finding it before he's had his fill.

It was Andrew's idea to embark upon *Midnight Snacks,* since he fancies himself a grandmaster of the eating game and also likes to cook. Having not entirely outgrown the frozen popsicle or the Twinkie, he has nonetheless discovered what other kids sometimes fail to appreciate: that the homemade snack is the ultimate pleasure.

A Word from the Son

To my way of thinking, one of the beauties of the midnight snack is that it has few of the cumbersome rules that are designed to "civilize" breakfast, lunch, and dinner. When you indulge in a snack, no one is going to insist that you indulge with a fork and a knife. Manners are out; fingers are in.

While "midnight" would seem to indicate a precise time for consuming this kind of treat, nothing could be further from our intentions. Unlike the three major meals, which tend to be scheduled, midnight snacks are spontaneous and can be enjoyed anytime under cover of darkness; come to think of it, they can be enjoyed anytime at all. Midnight should not be taken literally like four-o'clock tea. If it were, all the clandestine fun would vanish.

I first discovered the joys of the midnight snack before I was even capable of sneaking down to the refrigerator. This was back in the days when I was confined to a crib and hadn't yet mastered the art of walking. So when I got this craving for something like my milk bottle in the middle of the night, I had to bawl my eyes out to get assistance. Nowadays I find midnight snacks to be much less complicated.

While Mom might cast an embarrassed glance over her shoulder as she nudges an overflowing shopping cart down Aisle 12, I personally feel a sense of honor doing the shopping with two crowded carts in tow. People may shoot a quick stare of astonishment as I pass them, and may even think of Visigoths or orphanages. But I am always on the verge of boasting, "No sir, no ma'am, this is just for a family of four."

When I arrive home with the groceries, however, I can be sure to hear it from Mom, whose money I have just spent. "Honey, how could you spend so much on groceries when you and Doug are going back to college in a week?" she may say disapprovingly. Nonetheless, all the food does seem to evaporate by the time we leave. "Sweetie, who is going to eat these things? Délices au Chocolat imported from France . . . and they are so expensive!" she may cry out. Despite all this fuss, it is not infrequently that I happen to find her in the kitchen around midnight, munching on a Délice au Chocolat. I say, "I thought you didn't like those things," and she mutters, "Well, there's nothing else to eat."

When we put our heads together to pick our favorite midnight snacks and invent some new ones, we began to see some common threads: the best ones tend to involve "comfort foods"—cheese, sweets, peanut butter, bananas, nothing too hard on the stomach or too exotic. But since I've been in college, I've become acquainted with an entirely new category of midnight snack, one that addresses the plight of the all-nighter. The circumstances are clearly less than desirable (the realization that it's going to take the rest of the night to prepare for this final or finish that paper or make the final deadline for this book). But food at midnight, preferably caffeine-laden or five-alarm-spicy in this case, makes the night all the more endurable. I like to call this kind of midnight snack "food as a wake-up call."

A WORD ABOUT THIS BOOK

We discovered that our recipes fall into two categories: those that can be made on the spot when hunger strikes and those that can or should be made ahead in a spare quarter of an hour, in anticipation of the next attack. To accommodate the urge for instant gratification, we developed some ground rules. To qualify, a recipe must:

1. Have no more than six ingredients,
2. Use no more than two cooking utensils,
3. Take no more than fifteen minutes to make,

—and—

4. Whoever makes it cleans it up.

Naturally we reserve the right to break our own rules now and then.

Since midnight snacking is largely a solitary pleasure, the on-the-spot recipes are designed for single servings, but they're easy to multiply if you have company. The do-aheads are a bit more complex and make a larger amount; as long as you're going to the trouble, you might as well have some for the next time.

The exception is the "Breakfast at Midnight" chapter. These are sociable recipes, intended as the perfect nightcap for energetic evenings of dancing, skating, skiing, and so will serve two to four. They're designed to be eaten right away, but because we assume your companions will help you, they take a little more time to make.

One final consideration: a skeptical friend or two has asked us why we're *bothering* to write a midnight snack cookbook. "When I get hungry at night, I just go down and stick my hand in the cookie jar," they say. Well, we do that occasionally ourselves. But as good as some "old standard" packaged snacks may be, even Häagen Dazs coffee ice cream gets boring after a while. *Midnight Snacks* offers a great deal of variety without much fuss. We've tried to make the recipes interesting enough to appeal to real cooks, and simple enough to appeal to noncooks and lazy people. And while midnight is *our* hour of preference for snacking, you're on your own. Just as someone may have already tipped you off that it really *is* okay to rip the "Do Not Remove" tags off new pillows, we are hereby giving you license to use this book ANYTIME YOU PLEASE!

We would like to thank the following friends and family members for their generosity in giving us ideas, recipes, and/or reactions: Maya Angelou, Michelle Brien, Alice and Dave Cadwell, Mary Eitingon, Don Ernstein, Raoul Garcia, Rachel Jerman, Lynne Kilheffer, David Marshall, the late Barbara Melcher, Joan MacD. Miller, John Miller, Leonore Miller, Michelle Miller, Elysabeth Moras, Doug Schneider, Rhoda Schneider, Lottchen Shivers, Bee Simont, Steve Wallace, and Janet Watson. Special thanks must go to Carla Glasser, for her advice and enthusiasm; to Roy Finamore, for his expert guidance and good humor (and in spite of the fact that he insisted upon popcorn); to Leyla Morrissey, for her cheerful help and computer bailouts; to all the folks at Crown and Potter who brought the book into the world, including Lauren Shakely, Steve Magnuson, Joan de Mayo, Patty Eddy, Andrew Martin, Barbara Marks, Tina Constable, and designer Renato Stanisic; and especially to Michelle Sidrane, for going with the glow. Also thanks to Harry Moses, who tried so hard; and to Eric Schneider, who was the only one at home to taste and test and who turned out to be really good at both.

—Carol Schneider
—Andrew Schneider

IN THE NIGHT KITCHEN

With a nod to Maurice Sendak, here's a list of what <u>we</u> like to find in our kitchen in the wee hours. We're going to assume that you always have the most basic foods, such as eggs, flour, sugar, butter, mayonnaise, and so forth. Consider this a shopping list of essentials for the midnight prowler, in no particular order:

Apples
Bananas
A variety of cheeses
Peanut butter
Baking chocolate and
  chocolate chips
Cocoa powder
Maple syrup
Homemade-type jams

Cream cheese
Sour cream
Yogurt
A variety of nuts
Popcorn
Graham crackers
Potatoes
Salsa

A Few Words About Ingredients

★ If snacking is to remain spontaneous and easy, some of the rules of finer cooking have to be bent. Many baking recipes call for unsalted **butter** plus salt, but this is just a nuisance unless you're used to stocking it regularly. Since we always have lightly salted butter or margarine on hand, we just use what we have and cut out the salt.

★ For the same reason (convenience), all of our recipes that use **eggs** are designed for extra-large eggs, since that's what we always have in the house.

★ For serious cooking, **bouillon cubes** are not an acceptable substitute for chicken stock. But at midnight they're just fine. We think that Knorr makes the best of the lot. Remember that they tend to be very salty, so taste what you're making before adding any salt.

★ We don't want to open a 6-ounce can of **tomato paste** just to use a teaspoon or two. So we buy the kind that comes in a tube, available at many specialty-food stores.

★ We think it's nice to have a variety of **nuts** on hand for snacking or snack recipes, but we store them in the freezer so they won't turn rancid.

★ We like to snip **fresh herbs** like parsley, dill, and cilantro with scissors, which we keep in the kitchen for that purpose. Just scrunch a handful in one hand and snip with the other.

★ Certain convenience foods are worth keeping around. You don't have to stoop to pudding mixes and instant mashed potatoes, but **presifted flour, packaged graham cracker crumbs,** and even **canned diced tomatoes** (instead of whole or crushed) will save you time when you're in the grip of a snack attack. **Dehydrated minced onion** and **parsley flakes** are also useful.

PERMANENT FIXTURES

These are recipes for spreads, sauces, and other tasty, easy things to make ahead and have on hand as the basic building blocks for midnight snacks. They include sauces and relishes that make leftovers taste better—and dishes that make great leftovers. Some may quibble with our decision to put gingersnaps or meat loaf in the "permanent" category, but it's our book and we get to include those things that we can't live without.

SANDWICH SPREADS

Meat sandwiches—even good leftover meat sandwiches—get *so* boring after a while. But you can jazz them up with a variety of interesting spreads, some of which are also wonderful with other cold cuts, seafood, tomatoes, and so on. Unless otherwise noted, the recipes make just enough for one generous sandwich.

If you're concerned about fat and cholesterol, you can easily substitute lowfat mayonnaise, cream cheese, and sour cream in these recipes. The spreads are so highly flavored that you'll never notice the difference.

PESTO MAYO

Mix together *3 tablespoons mayonnaise* and *1 teaspoon summer or winter pesto* (pages 20, 21). Blend well. This is especially good with turkey, chicken, roast beef, and tomatoes.

APRICOT CHUTNEY MUSTARD

Measure out *1 tablespoon mango chutney* and dice any large chunks. Add *2 tablespoons apricot preserves* and *½ teaspoon Dijon mustard.* Stir well. We love this with ham, salami, and other smoked meats.

MAYONNAISE PROVENÇAL
MAKES ABOUT ³/₄ CUP

In a food processor, place *2 tablespoons chopped pimientos; 2 tablespoons pitted black olives, halved; 1 tablespoon capers; and 2 tablespoons freshly snipped parsley.* Spin until chopped and blended. Transfer to a small bowl or jar, and mix well with *½ cup mayonnaise.* This is great with meat loaf, pot roast, and ham.

HORSERADISH CREAM

Mix together *1 tablespoon mayonnaise, 1 tablespoon sour cream,* and *1½ teaspoons prepared horseradish.* Blend well. A classic with roast beef and pot roast.

CURRY MAYONNAISE

Mix *¼ teaspoon curry powder* with *3 tablespoons mayonnaise* and *a drop or two of lemon juice.* Add *1 tablespoon minced celery* and *1 tablespoon minced banana or apple* and stir well. Try this with sliced chicken or turkey. Or cut leftover poultry into chunks and toss with this spread to make a quick chicken or turkey salad.

ONION-DILL CREAM

Place *2 tablespoons cream cheese* and *1 tablespoon sour cream or yogurt* in a cup; beat vigorously with a spoon to blend and soften. Add *½ teaspoon dehydrated minced onion* and *1 teaspoon freshly snipped dill.* Stir well. This is especially good with garden-fresh tomato slices or grated carrots. Yes, as a sandwich. Try it!

SPICY SANTA FE MAYONNAISE
MAKES 1 CUP

This is a little more trouble, so the recipe makes a decent-size batch. It will keep for about a week in the refrigerator.

Mix well *1 cup mayonnaise, ¾ teaspoon ground cumin, l tablespoon minced red bell pepper, 1 jalapeño pepper, seeded and minced, 1 tablespoon minced scallion,* and *1 tablespoon freshly snipped cilantro.* Try this with lobster, lump crabmeat, any leftover seafood, and almost any sandwich meat.

CRAN/RAS/ORANGE RELISH

Mix together *2 tablespoons whole-berry cranberry sauce, 1 tablespoon homemade-style (meaning thick) raspberry preserves,* and *½ teaspoon grated orange rind.* Blend well. This is good with fowl.

SUMMER PESTO

In summer, when you have access to fresh basil in quantity, make several batches of pesto at a time and store them in leftover half-pound margarine containers. It will keep indefinitely—literally, for years—in the freezer. We kid around about the vintage when we take them out: "1992? Oh yeah, that was a good year!"

MAKES 1 CUP

3 cups well-washed, tightly packed fresh basil leaves
1 garlic clove, peeled and halved
4 tablespoons (½ stick) butter or margarine
¼ cup olive oil
1 teaspoon salt
¼ cup chopped freshly snipped parsley
½ cup grated Parmesan cheese
¼ cup pine nuts (optional)

Place all the ingredients in a food processor and process, scraping down the sides with a spatula if necessary, for 2 or 3 minutes or until a thick purée is formed.

NOTE: This amount of pesto will coat 2 pounds of spaghetti or other pasta. But don't be so hidebound! It can enliven midnight snacks or leftovers. Keep a thawed container of pesto in the fridge and use a dollop on heated leftover potatoes, or in vegetable soup to jazz it up. Try spreading a little on leftover fish or chicken before heating it in the microwave. And check out the Pesto Mayo on page 18.

WINTER PESTO

This parsley-walnut sauce is one of the most popular items on the autumn menu of the Boiler Room Café in Great Barrington, Massachusetts. With fresh parsley available all winter long, it's a wonderful pick-me-up for roasted vegetables or pasta.

Unlike its summer cousin, this pesto cannot be stored for long periods of time. It's best when freshly made, and will keep in the refrigerator for only a couple of days.

MAKES 1¼ CUPS

1 cup shelled walnuts
2 cups washed, stemmed, and firmly packed parsley
1 tablespoon chopped garlic
1 teaspoon kosher salt
Pinch of freshly ground pepper
¾ cup extra-virgin olive oil

Lightly toast the walnuts in the oven or a toaster oven; set aside to cool completely.

Spin parsley briefly in a food processor; then add walnuts, garlic, salt, and pepper. Pulse until coarsely blended. While the machine is running, add olive oil. Store in a tightly closed container.

CADWELL'S CORNER MEAT LOAF

Cadwell's Corner is a wonderful breakfast-and-lunch café in the foothills of the Berkshires in Cornwall, Connecticut. We're grateful to Alice and Dave Cadwell for sharing the recipe for their much-praised meat loaf, which has overtones of Alice's Armenian heritage.

Any serious snacker knows that leftover meat loaf is a staple of the midnight kitchen, largely because it's even better the next day (or later that night) in a sandwich. This one is no exception.

MAKES 1 9×5-INCH LOAF

8 slices good-quality oatmeal bread
¾ cup buttermilk
2½ pounds ground sirloin
3 garlic cloves, peeled and crushed
1 cup freshly snipped parsley
1 tablespoon ground cumin
1 tablespoon dried oregano
1 tablespoon dried basil
1 tablespoon Tabasco sauce
2 tablespoons soy sauce
1 teaspoon ground cinnamon
1 teaspoon ground allspice
½ cup ketchup
1 egg
Salt and freshly ground pepper to taste

Preheat oven to 375°.

Tear bread slices into small pieces, or use a food processor to make bread crumbs. Place in a large bowl and pour buttermilk over; squeeze with your hands until it is absorbed.

Add all the other ingredients, and knead with your hands until blended. Do not overwork or the loaf will be tough and too tightly packed. Mound the mixture in a large (9 × 5 × 3-inch) loaf pan, and bake for 1 hour and 20 minutes.

SLIGHTLY SPICY TOMATO SAUCE

This sauce freezes well and is good to have on hand for either freshly made or leftover spaghetti or other pasta.

MAKES 3 CUPS

In a saucepan heat *1 tablespoon olive oil.* Add *1 or 2 garlic cloves, minced,* and sauté for a minute or two. Add *1 28-ounce can (3 cups) crushed tomatoes, 1 tablespoon tomato paste, 1 dried red pepper, crumbled (or a pinch of crushed red pepper),* and *a handful of freshly snipped parsley.* Cook at a high simmer for about 10 minutes, or until the mixture has thickened. Add *salt and pepper to taste.*

VARIATION: Try adding 1 can of tuna, drained.

FLAVORED BUTTERS

These butters play the same role as the sandwich spreads: They make leftovers and ordinary sandwiches more appealing. They have applications for regular meals as well, indicated at the end of each recipe. The first two must be whipped in an electric mixer; the last two can be mixed by hand if the butter is at room temperature. And margarine—even light margarine—can be substituted in any of these recipes.

You can store these butters in small custard cups. In case you have snacking company and decide to sit down for a change—or if you use the butters at dinner—the cups make nice containers to bring to the table.

SHALLOT/PARSLEY BUTTER

Cream *½ cup (1 stick) butter* in an electric mixer until light and fluffy. Add *1 tablespoon minced shallots, 2 tablespoons freshly snipped parsley,* and *salt and pepper to taste.* Slowly beat in *1½ tablespoons lemon juice* until absorbed. Chill. Try it with steaks, hamburgers, grilled cheese sandwiches, boiled potatoes, and green vegetables.

BALSAMIC/MUSTARD BUTTER

Cream *½ cup (1 stick) butter* in an electric mixer until light and fluffy. Beat in *1 tablespoon Dijon mustard* and, slowly, *1 tablespoon balsamic vinegar.* Add *salt and pepper to taste.* Chill. This is good with ham and cheese sandwiches, steak, and roast beef.

PESTO BUTTER

Combine *½ cup (1 stick) softened butter* with *1 tablespoon summer or winter pesto* (pages 20, 21) and blend well. Chill. We love this on cheese and tomato sandwiches, Cheese Waffles (page 65), and baked or boiled potatoes.

ORANGE/CINNAMON BUTTER

Combine *½ cup (1 stick) softened butter* with *2 teaspoons freshly grated orange rind, ½ teaspoon ground cinnamon,* and *2 teaspoons sugar.* Chill. Spread this on toasted wheat bread, Pecan or Chocolate Waffles (pages 64–65), and many kinds of crackers.

JOAN'S HOT FUDGE SAUCE

MAKES 1½ CUPS

In the top of a double boiler over simmering water, heat *1 cup sugar, ⅔ cup heavy cream, 2 ounces unsweetened chocolate,* and *a pinch of salt* until the chocolate is melted. Remove from the heat, and add *1 teaspoon vanilla* and *2 tablespoons butter or margarine.* Stir until well blended.

LYNNE KILHEFFER'S LEMON CURD

This is an unconventional way to make lemon curd—grating the rind coarsely, then straining it out—but it's much faster than grating the lemons on a fine blade.

MAKES 3 CUPS

4 lemons
6 eggs, beaten
2 cups sugar
½ cup (1 stick) butter

Grate the rinds of the lemons on the coarse blade of a grater; then squeeze out the juice. In the top of a double boiler, combine grated rind, juice, eggs, and sugar, and cook over boiling water, stirring constantly.

Just as the mixture starts to thicken (this will take 5 to 10 minutes), remove it from the heat and pour it through a strainer to remove the rind. Pour the mixture back into the top of the double boiler and continue cooking for a few minutes more, until it is fully thickened. Add butter and stir well to melt.

Cool, then chill. The lemon curd will thicken further as it cools.

EASY MICROWAVE APPLE BUTTER

Make this in the autumn, when you can get freshly picked apples at farm stands and orchards. Northern Spy, McIntosh, and Cortland are all good varieties for this recipe.

MAKES 2¼ CUPS

½ cup granulated sugar
½ cup firmly packed dark brown sugar
½ teaspoon ground cinnamon
¼ teaspoon ground cloves
¼ teaspoon ground allspice
Pinch of ground nutmeg
2 pounds cooking apples, peeled and cored

Mix sugars and spices in a small mixing bowl. Cut apples into eighths, and place in a 1-quart microwave dish. Sprinkle the sugar mixture on top; toss gently to blend. Cover tightly with plastic wrap.

Microwave on high for 15 minutes. Remove from the oven and carefully empty the mixture into a food processor. Blend for a few seconds, until the apple butter is uniformly pulpy.

Let the mixture cool, and then store in tightly covered jars in the refrigerator. It should keep for up to 3 months.

MOKIES

You don't need an electric mixer for these dark mocha brownies.

MAKES 16 2-INCH SQUARES

¾ cup (1½ sticks) butter or margarine
2 ounces unsweetened chocolate
3 tablespoons instant coffee
1 cup sugar
2 eggs
1 teaspoon vanilla
1 cup flour
½ teaspoon baking powder
1 cup (8 ounces) semisweet chocolate chips

Preheat oven to 350°.

Carefully heat butter, chocolate, and coffee in a small heavy-bottomed pan over low heat, stirring until just melted and smooth. (Or microwave on high in an appropriate dish for 2 minutes or until butter is melted; then stir until chocolate is completely melted.)

Transfer to a large mixing bowl and add sugar. Mix in eggs and vanilla until well blended. Stir in flour and baking powder and mix well; then fold in chocolate chips.

Spread the batter evenly in a greased 9-inch-square pan and bake for 35 minutes, or until a toothpick inserted in the center comes out relatively clean (try not to stick it into a chocolate chip!).

GINGERSNAPS

This is a disobedient, and slightly spicier, version of the Ginger Thins recipe in *The Joy of Cooking*. It disobeys the instructions to bake tiny ⅛-inch "dots" of dough since "they toughen if they are larger." I have not found that to be the case, and if you make larger cookies and just bake them a bit longer, they are perfectly tender and the whole process is a lot less tedious.

MAKES ABOUT 100 2- OR 3-INCH COOKIES

¾ *cup (1½ sticks) butter or margarine*
1 cup firmly packed dark brown sugar
1 egg
¼ *cup molasses*
1½ cups flour
½ *teaspoon baking soda*
¾ *teaspoon ground ginger*
½ *teaspoon ground cinnamon*
½ *teaspoon ground cloves*

Preheat oven to 325°.

Cream together butter and brown sugar with a mixer until fluffy. Add egg and molasses, and blend well. Sift together the remaining ingredients. Add sifted dry ingredients gradually to the creamed mixture, beating at low speed until blended.

Drop the batter by the heaping half-teaspoon 1 inch apart onto greased cookie sheets, and bake 7 minutes or until browned. Cool for several minutes on the cookie sheets, then remove to racks.

MIDNIGHT SAVORIES

There are two basic kinds of snackers. The most common are probably those with a sweet tooth, who see main courses as a necessary evil on the way to dessert and who always crave a sweet at midnight. But the others know the siren song of a good bread with cheese, or an aromatic homemade soup. In the spirit of the latter, we have compiled an array of easy savory recipes. And in the time-honored tradition of eating your dinner before your dessert, we're offering the savory snacks first.

THE ORIGINAL MIDNIGHT SNACK, UPDATED

If Louis XIV's courtiers took plates of sweet peas to their chambers at midnight, how might we translate that snack today? Perhaps with some sugar snap peas, which now seem to be in the markets almost all year 'round, and a dip?

BJ's Paprika–Red Onion Dip

Mix together some *cream cheese* and *sour cream* (you can thin the mixture with a little *milk*, if desired). Add some *minced red onion* and enough *paprika* to make the dip pink.

QUICK HOMEMADE SOUPS

If you're not in the mood for sweets, nothing soothes at midnight quite like a mug of thick, steaming soup. It's amazing how quickly you can make a single serving of soup from leftovers, and it's so much better than opening a can. Here are three ideas to start you off. Once you get the hang of it, you can make substitutions and invent your own.

Thick Vegetable Soup

In a blender, purée *½ cup chopped cooked cauliflower or broccoli, ½ cup cooked rice, noodles, or chopped potatoes, ½ cup chicken broth or bouillon,* and *¼ cup plain yogurt or buttermilk.* Pour into a mug and microwave on high for 2½ minutes. Add some *chopped fresh parsley or other herbs* and *salt and pepper to taste.*

NOTE: When you blend the vegetables, don't go too far—leaving a little texture will make the soup more interesting.

CREAM OF TOMATO SOUP

For this recipe, remember to buy a tube, rather than a can, of tomato paste. You can use a teaspoon or two, put the top back on, and keep it indefinitely.

In a mug, combine *1½ teaspoons tomato paste* and *¼ teaspoon sugar* and stir very well. Add *¾ cup tomato or V-8 juice, 1 scallion, chopped,* and *¼ cup leftover rice or orzo or other small noodles,* and mix together. Microwave on high for 2½ minutes. Stir in *¼ cup sour cream* and blend well. Add some *chopped fresh dill.*

CURRIED WINTER SQUASH SOUP

Use leftovers here, or thaw a box of frozen puréed squash. Some good substitutes for the squash are leftover cooked carrots or sweet potatoes, and canned pumpkin purée. If your leftover vegetables are not already puréed, mix all the ingredients in a blender.

In a mug, combine *⅔ cup puréed winter squash* with *½ teaspoon curry powder (or to taste)* and stir well. Add *⅓ cup chicken broth or bouillon, ¼ cup applesauce,* and *a sprinkle of garlic powder.* Add some *diced apple* or *chopped fresh cilantro,* if desired, and microwave on high for 2½ minutes.

NOTE: Maya Angelou, who is a wonderful cook as well as a gifted writer, has a good idea for saving and using the cooking juices from a roasted chicken: Cool sufficiently so that the fat can be skimmed off, then store in ice cube trays in the freezer. Use as needed in place of chicken broth or bouillon.

CRACKER-COOKIE COMBOS

These don't even deserve to be called recipes because they're so simple and quick. Consider them *ideas* that can be mixed and matched.

SPREAD . . .	ON OR BETWEEN TWO . . .
Cream cheese	*Gingersnaps (page 29)*
Lemon Curd (page 26)	*Oatcakes*
	Wheatmeal biscuits
Blackberry jam	*Imported plain salted crackers*
Apple Butter (page 27)	*Graham crackers*
Peanut Sauce (page 54)	*Arrowroot crackers*
Orange/Cinnamon Butter (page 25)	*Wheat Thins*
	Chocolate wafers
Semisweet chocolate chips	*Saltines*

Our friend Lottchen Shivers keeps a package of saltines and a bag of chocolate chips in her desk drawer at work and sprinkles some chips on a cracker when she gets the urge. We made fun of her when we first discovered this curious habit, but we've had to wipe those smiles off our faces because it really works. There's something about that salty-sweet combination that is very basic to snack satisfaction.

OPEN-FACED
SANDWICH COMBOS

SPREAD . . .

*Apple Butter (page 27)
and leftover turkey slices*

*Cream cheese and white
radish slices*

*Garden-fresh tomatoes
and melted Brie*

Meat loaf (page 22)

*Avocado slices, watercress,
pimientos, Muenster cheese*

*Peanut sauce (page 54)
and bacon*

Tuna salad with apple chunks

ON . . .

Toasted oatmeal bread

Russian black bread

Onion-dill bread

Lavash

Pita bread

Toasted rye

Sour cream bread

If the choice of breads sounds a bit fanciful, it's because we're spoiled—we own a bread machine. It's an indispensable piece of equipment for anyone who loves to snack because your part of the process (as opposed to the machine's) takes less than 5 minutes. What its product lacks in variety of shape or crust is well made up for by its homey texture and the incredible range of recipes that have been developed for it.

A TRIO OF QUICKLY COOKED CHEESE SNACKS

These can all be done in a toaster oven.

JOHN'S GRILLED CHEESE WITH JAM

Lightly toast *2 slices bread* and spread with *strawberry jam.* Place *2 slices of Swiss cheese* on top, and broil until cheese melts and starts to color.

DAVID'S WHEATA PITAS

Cut *1 whole-wheat pita bread* in quarters, then split apart. Spread each triangle with *soft margarine* and sprinkle with *coarsely grated Parmesan cheese* to taste. Place on a cookie sheet under the broiler until cheese is golden and edges of bread are crisp.

VARIATION: For variety, use flavored butters (page 24), or use cinnamon sugar instead of cheese.

CHEDDAR CHEESE AND CHUTNEY

Measure out *2 tablespoons Major Grey–type chutney* and dice any large chunks. Add *4 tablespoons port wine cheddar spread* (available in most supermarkets) and mix well. Spread on *2 slices toast,* cut in half on the diagonal, and broil until cheese mixture bubbles and starts to color.

NOTE: These make great hors d'oeuvres: Before spreading the cheese mixture, cut each slice of toast on both diagonals to make four triangles. Then broil as described above.

THREE WAYS TO DO POPCORN

One of the greatest boons to the midnight snacker is microwave popcorn: no time, no fuss, no utensils except the bowl it's served in, and no calories to speak of (unless of course you do what we are proposing here). The trouble is, it gets boring. So try some toppings. The ones below are sufficient to coat *four cups of popcorn,* and be sure to use the "natural flavor" type. (The usual microwave package yields about two quarts, or eight cups, so you could actually try two different toppings by dividing the batch in half.) Don't make the mistake of thinking the more topping, the better; any more topping than this will make the popcorn soggy.

ANDREW'S WAY
Toss with *2 tablespoons melted butter or margarine* and *2 tablespoons finely grated cheese.* (Hard cheese, such as Parmesan, is the easiest to grate finely, but some softer cheeses such as extra-sharp cheddar have a stronger flavor.)

ROY'S WAY
Melt *2 tablespoons butter or margarine* in a frying pan. Add *1 teaspoon curry powder* and cook a minute or so. Toss with the popcorn. You could add a handful of raisins.

LEYLA'S WAY
Toss with *2 tablespoons melted butter or margarine* mixed with ½ *teaspoon chili paste.*

STUFFED POTATOES

Potatoes baked in a conventional oven have a better, fluffier consistency than those baked in a microwave. But if you're going to mash them anyway, as you will in this recipe, nothing beats the microwave for instant gratification. Stuffed potatoes take a few minutes longer than plain baked potatoes, but they're so much more interesting. And you've saved all that time by using the microwave.

Scrub an *8-ounce baking potato* and prick once or twice with a fork. Microwave, uncovered, on high for 7 to 10 minutes, depending upon the size of your oven. Carefully remove the potato from the oven with a potholder, and cut a thin slice off the top. With a spoon, remove the pulp, leaving a $\frac{1}{4}$-inch-thick shell. In a small bowl (a cereal bowl works well), mash the pulp with a fork. Beat in any of the following:

- ★ *a pat of butter and a tablespoon of milk*
- ★ *a pat of butter and $\frac{1}{2}$ teaspoon summer or winter pesto (pages 20, 21)*
- ★ *a pat of butter, $\frac{1}{2}$ teaspoon chili powder, and $\frac{1}{3}$ cup grated sharp cheese*
- ★ *1 tablespoon Onion-Dill Cream or Horseradish Cream (both page 19)*
- ★ *a pat of butter and 1 tablespoon leftover creamed spinach*
- ★ *$1\frac{1}{2}$ tablespoons of any of the savory flavored butters on pages 24–25*

Add *salt and pepper* as desired, and heap the mixture back into the potato shell. The process takes such a short time that you shouldn't have to reheat the potato. If you want, sprinkle a little grated cheese on top (if it works with the stuffing) and run it under the broiler to brown it.

STUFFED YAMS
Prepare and bake an *8-ounce sweet potato or yam* as for a white potato (see opposite page; it will need several more minutes in the microwave). Mash the pulp with *1 tablespoon butter, 1 teaspoon maple syrup,* and *salt and pepper to taste.* If you have any of the following around, you can also fold them in: bacon bits, diced dried fruit, toasted blanched almonds, or a bit of coconut.

CREAMY POLENTA

Empty *2 packets of instant grits* into a widemouthed soup bowl and add *1 cup milk;* stir. Microwave on high for 2 minutes, and stir again. Immediately stir in *1 tablespoon butter or margarine* and *2 tablespoons heavy cream.* You can season with *salt and pepper* if you want, but it's really not necessary.

Serve with any of the following toppings:
* ★ *thin slices of fontina cheese, laid on top of steaming polenta so they will melt*
* ★ *a small dollop of summer or winter pesto (pages 20, 21)*
* ★ *a small dollop of Slightly Spicy Tomato Sauce (page 23)*
* ★ *all of the above*

MIDNIGHT SWEETS

It's hard to find many sweets that meet our "instant gratification" ground rules, so most of these recipes are do-aheads. You'll find that preparing them in some spare moments or over the weekend is similar to making a good investment: prudent, long-term, and ultimately extremely rewarding.

HASTY PUDDINGS

Puddings, with their aura of regression and childhood, are the perfect comfort food for midnight. It's not really practical to make single servings, but we've never known them to last very long if there are multiple portions. Someone will eat them. Probably you.

FRUITY TAPIOCA
MAKES 4 SERVINGS

Whisk together *⅓ cup sugar, 3 tablespoons instant tapioca, 2½ cups milk,* and *1 egg* in a heavy saucepan and let stand for 5 minutes to soften the tapioca. Cook, stirring, until the mixture comes to a full boil. Remove from the heat and stir in *½ teaspoon almond extract* and *2 cups cubed fresh peaches or nectarines.* The pudding will thicken as it cools; you can serve it warm or cold.

NOTE: Many other fruits work equally well: raspberries, blueberries, cubed strawberries or bananas, or a mixture. Depending upon the fruit you choose, you may want to adjust the amount of sugar or to substitute 1 teaspoon vanilla for the almond extract. If you want a richer pudding, you can substitute heavy cream for 1 cup of the milk.

COFFEE CUSTARD
MAKES 4 SERVINGS

This baked pudding takes a long time in the oven, but almost no time at all to put together.

Preheat oven to 300°.

In a blender, place *1 cup strong hot coffee (or decaf), 5 tablespoons sugar, 1 cup milk, a pinch of salt, 2 eggs,* and *1 teaspoon vanilla.* Blend well, and divide the mixture among four custard cups. Place the cups inside a 9-inch baking pan and pour hot (not boiling) water halfway up the sides of the cups. Bake for 1 hour, or until a knife inserted near the edge of a cup comes out clean (the center will set by the time it cools). Remove the cups from the pan and cool on a rack; then chill.

VARIATION: You can make a mocha custard by adding 3 tablespoons unsweetened cocoa powder and 1 tablespoon butter or margarine to the blender at the very beginning.

DEADLINE BLONDIES

We defy you to find a faster dessert baked from scratch. Our contribution is adapted from a late-Forties elementary school fundraiser cookbook, for which children were asked to bring in their favorite family recipes. This one shows up twice, under two different names, which proves either that the editor was not paying attention or that it was a very popular recipe. Or both.

Use packaged graham cracker crumbs for maximum speed. You can add ½ cup chopped nuts or flaked coconut if you wish.

MAKES 16 2-INCH SQUARES

Preheat oven to 350°. In a mixing bowl, combine *1 14-ounce can sweetened condensed milk, 2 cups graham cracker crumbs, 1 6-ounce package semisweet chocolate chips,* and *1 teaspoon vanilla.* Spread immediately (the mixture thickens upon standing and becomes hard to handle) in a greased 9-inch square baking pan. Bake for 15 minutes.

THINGS DIPPED IN WHITE CHOCOLATE

You may have noticed that you don't see anything called "white chocolate" on supermarket shelves anymore, although you do see sweets named Swiss White Confectionery Bar, Creamy White Bar, Vanilla Milk Chips, and White Pastilles. That's because the FDA is currently reviewing a petition brought by the chocolate industry to reserve this designation for the real McCoy—which contains fats derived from cacao—as opposed to imitations, which are made from cheaper ingredients. For the purposes of this recipe, you can use either the real or the mock.

Melt *4 tablespoons (½ stick) butter or margarine* and *3 ounces white chocolate* in the top of a double boiler over hot (not boiling) water, stirring to blend. Pour into a custard cup, cool, and use as a dipping sauce. These are a few of our favorite "things":

Medium-size twisted pretzels
Gingersnaps (page 29)
Whole strawberries
Banana chunks
Navel orange segments
Thick breadsticks broken into pieces

Dipping works much better when you cool the sauce for half an hour and use that time to freeze the items you're going to coat. Use a pincer for the pretzels so that the entire pretzel is coated; with the other items, dip so that only half or two thirds is covered. Shake off any excess sauce and place on a wax paper–covered cake rack to dry. If they are not eaten soon after drying, the chocolate-coated items should be stored in the refrigerator (the chocolate will "sweat" if left at room temperature).

CARAMEL NUT GRAHAMS

Here is the exception that proves the rule: a quick sweet snack that can be made for one person. These caramel grahams are better with butter, healthier with margarine. You choose.

MAKES 1 SERVING

Preheat toaster oven to 400°.

Melt *1 tablespoon butter or margarine* in a small saucepan. Add *1 tablespoon light brown sugar* and cook, stirring, over medium heat for a minute or two, until the sugar has melted and the mixture is thickened and smooth. With a teaspoon, spread the caramel mixture over *4 or 5 graham cracker squares.* Sprinkle with some *chopped nuts (pecans, walnuts, or sliced blanched almonds)* and bake in the toaster oven for 4 to 5 minutes, until the topping is bubbly and starting to brown. Cool.

MAPLE-ALMOND CRISPS

To get the full flavor of these cookies, only the genuine item will do—don't use ersatz "pancake syrup." We use Grade B maple syrup—it's darker, stronger flavored, and less expensive than Grade A syrup.

MAKES 4 DOZEN COOKIES

½ cup (1 stick) butter or margarine
1 cup firmly packed dark brown sugar
½ cup pure maple syrup
½ teaspoon vanilla
1 egg
1½ cups sifted flour
2 teaspoons baking powder
½ teaspoon salt
1 cup sliced blanched almonds

Preheat oven to 375°.

Using an electric mixer, cream together butter and brown sugar. Add maple syrup, vanilla, and egg, and beat until smooth.

Combine flour, baking powder, and salt and add to the batter, beating well. Stir in almonds. Drop by teaspoons onto greased baking sheets and bake for 10 to 12 minutes, or until the edges are brown. Remove *immediately* from the baking sheets, or they will stick. Allow the cookies to cool on racks.

LEONORE'S FAMOUS SILKY FUDGE

Well, famous in a few families, anyway.

No self-respecting snack cookbook should be without a fudge recipe, and we think this is one of the best, even if it does owe a debt to the Marshmallow Fluff jar. It's a lot simpler than the old-fashioned candy-thermometer method, and somewhat healthier too, since it contains no heavy cream. It's fudge for people who like their fudge straight and simple, with no nuts interfering with their pure chocolate pleasure.

MAKES 64 1-INCH SQUARES

In a heavy-bottomed saucepan place *2 cups sugar, 4 tablespoons (½ stick) butter or margarine, ¾ cup evaporated milk, 1 small jar (7½ ounces) Marshmallow Fluff,* and *½ teaspoon salt.* Stir over low heat until well blended. Bring to a boil, then continue to boil slowly, stirring constantly, for 5 minutes; the mixture will turn golden. Remove from the heat and stir in *12 ounces fine imported semisweet chocolate,* broken into chunks, and *1 teaspoon vanilla.* Stir until smooth. Turn into a buttered 9-inch square baking pan. Cool, then chill. With a sharp knife, cut the fudge into inch-square portions, and remove from the pan. Wrap in aluminum foil and store in the refrigerator or freezer.

NOTE: If you try to measure Marshmallow Fluff, you'll just get all gooped up. Better to buy the small jar if you are making this amount of fudge, or the big one if you want to make a double recipe.

ANDREW'S IMPORTED ODDBALL CONFECTIONS

These white chocolate–chunk cookies are neither imported nor particularly oddball, but they earned their name when Andrew started doing the family grocery shopping. The price I paid for being relieved of this task was an extra $20 per trip in the form of strange goodies that called out to him from the shelves, and which I labeled his "imported oddball confections." The appelation stuck, and when he created these cookies (in a bald-faced attempt to surpass Mrs. You-Know-Who), it seemed the obvious choice of name.

The amount of vanilla is not a misprint; it's the secret weapon.

MAKES ABOUT 3 DOZEN COOKIES

⅓ cup margarine
⅓ cup shortening
½ cup granulated sugar
½ cup firmly packed dark brown sugar
3 tablespoons vanilla
1 egg
1½ cups flour
½ teaspoon salt
1 teaspoon baking soda
7 ounces white chocolate

Preheat oven to 375°.

Beat margarine, shortening, sugars, and vanilla in an electric mixer until well blended. Beat in egg. Add flour, salt, and baking soda. Beat thoroughly. Break white chocolate into bite-size chunks and stir into dough. Use a tablespoon to drop the cookie dough onto ungreased cookie sheets. Bake for 8 to 10 minutes, or until light brown. Allow the cookies to cool on racks.

FRENCH YOGURT CAKE

My son Eric spent a summer with a French family and acquired this delicious recipe from his French "cousin" Elysabeth Moras. We think it's perfect for a snack cookbook since the empty yogurt container is your only measuring cup, meaning there's less to clean up.

MAKES 1 9×13-INCH CAKE

Preheat oven to 350°.

Empty *1 8-ounce container of plain yogurt* into the bowl of an electric mixer. Rinse and dry the container. Fill it 3 times with *sugar* and 3 times with *flour,* adding each containerful to the bowl. Beat on low speed. Add *3 eggs* and mix well. Add *1 teaspoon baking soda.* Fill yogurt container halfway with *corn oil.* Add and beat until the batter is smooth.

Pour the batter into a greased 9 × 13-inch baking pan, and bake for 50 minutes, or until a toothpick comes out clean.

NOTE: For extra interest, stir in 1 yogurt container of blueberries, chocolate chips, nuts, chopped banana or peach or apple, or any mixture of those, just before pouring the batter into the pan.

TWO MORE WAYS TO DO POPCORN

The two greatest instruments of torture in cooking, in our opinion, are the candy thermometer and the food mill. Most candied popcorn recipes call for the former, but we are rather proud of ourselves for developing two sweet popcorn recipes that avoid the dreaded instrument entirely.

Both offer a good way for using up leftover plain popcorn. The slight saltiness of microwave popcorn is actually an asset, assuming you share our fondness for sweet-salty combinations.

HEAVENLY POPCORN
MAKES ABOUT 1¼ POUNDS

This is the chocolate confection usually known as heavenly hash, with popcorn substituted for the nuts. Use the best-quality chocolate you can find.

Line a 9-inch baking pan with enough waxed paper so that the long sides overlap the edges of the pan. Have ready *1 cup popcorn* and *4 dozen miniature marshmallows.* Break *1 pound of semisweet chocolate* into eight pieces. Heat half of them in a covered microwaveable container for 2 minutes, stir, and heat for another 2 minutes. Remove from oven and stir until completely melted. Pour on top of waxed paper and spread evenly. Sprinkle popcorn and marshmallows evenly on top. Melt the remaining chocolate as above and drizzle as evenly as possible over popcorn and marshmallows.

Use the long edges of the waxed paper to pull candy out of the pan. Place on a rack and chill in the refrigerator, then break into pieces. Store in a tin lined with waxed paper in the refrigerator.

POPCORN-PECAN CLUSTERS
MAKES ABOUT 25 2-INCH CLUSTERS

In a bowl, toss *4 cups popcorn* with *1 cup chopped pecans.* Set aside. In a 3-quart heavy-bottomed pan, combine ⅔ *cup milk, 2 cups sugar,* and *2 tablespoons light corn syrup.* Bring to a boil and boil for 3 minutes without stirring; mixture will bubble up and more than double in volume. Remove from heat and add *6 tablespoons peanut butter* and *1 teaspoon vanilla.* Stir well. Pour over popcorn and pecans and toss until well combined. Drop by tablespoonfuls onto waxed paper spread on cookie sheets. Clusters will set as they cool.

A WHOLE CHAPTER ON PEANUT BUTTER

An informal poll has demonstrated that peanut butter is the vice of choice for midnight snackers. But aren't you tired of peanut butter with jelly or celery or—worse yet—sticking your finger straight into the peanut butter jar? Can you really tolerate Fluffernutters, those awful Sixties concoctions of spongy white bread, peanut butter, and marshmallow whose recipe is still on the Marshmallow Fluff jar? We respectfully submit some alternatives.

DON ERNSTEIN'S PEANUT SAUCE

Don Ernstein is the maestro of a Los Angeles catering company called Wonderful Parties, Wonderful Foods. This spicy dip lives up to his company's name and is great with crudités, particularly carrots. You can make it in seconds. You'll find the sweet chili sauce in Asian markets.

MAKES ¾ CUP

In a food processor, chop *4 ounces (¾ cup) dry-roasted peanuts* with *½ cup sweet chili sauce (without garlic)* until well blended but not completely smooth. Add *1 tablespoon dark sesame oil* and a little water to thin, if necessary.

NOTE: Try spreading a bit of this sauce on rye toast and topping it with crisp bacon slices.

SESAME NOODLES

This is an amalgam of two recipes—ours and our friend Rachel Jerman's. The ingredients aren't in everybody's cupboard, but they are easy to find at health food stores and Asian groceries if your supermarket doesn't carry them. And it's worth stocking up on them since the sesame sauce is so delicious and easy to make. It will also keep in the refrigerator for a week or two, so you can use what you need on small amounts of leftover spaghetti and save the rest for another night.

MAKES ENOUGH FOR 8 OUNCES OF NOODLES

¼ cup crunchy peanut butter
1½ tablespoons sesame oil
1½ tablespoons tahini (sesame seed paste)
¼ cup peanut oil
1 tablespoon soy sauce
1 tablespoon rice vinegar
1 teaspoon grated fresh ginger
Dash of Tabasco sauce
Salt and freshly ground pepper to taste

Throw all of the ingredients into a food processor and let 'er rip. That's it! Toss with cold or hot spaghetti or Chinese egg noodles. Garnish with sliced scallions and julienned red bell pepper if you have 'em and want 'em.

PEANUT BUTTER AND BANANA S'MORES

Forget the campfire, even forget the marshmallows, as good as they are; these s'mores can be made in the wink of an eye in the comfort of your own kitchen. The fudge sauce doesn't have to be hot, but use it sparingly; otherwise it will squish out all over you when you bite into this treat.

Spread *2 graham cracker squares* with *creamy peanut butter*. Place *4 thin slices of banana* on one of the crackers and drizzle with *fudge sauce* (page 25). Put the other cracker on top, and you're ready to roll.

PEANUT BUTTER APPLE

Our friend Steve Wallace suggested a peanut butter snack that had never occurred to us: take a *good eating apple* and pry out the core almost all the way to the bottom. Stuff with *peanut butter* (crunchy makes it more interesting), and munch away.

P.B. AND CHIPS

Your favorite Toll House cookie—with a peanut butter base. This may not look like enough chocolate chips, but if you put in too many, you begin to lose the peanutty taste of the cookie.

MAKES ABOUT 7 DOZEN 2-INCH COOKIES

1 cup (2 sticks) butter or margarine
1 cup crunchy peanut butter
1 cup granulated sugar
1 cup firmly packed light brown sugar
2 eggs
2 cups flour
1 teaspoon baking soda
1 6-ounce package semisweet chocolate chips

Preheat oven to 325°.

Using an electric mixer, cream butter and peanut butter. Gradually add sugars, and cream well. Add eggs, one at a time, and beat until smooth. Add flour and baking soda, and beat only until incorporated. Stir in chocolate chips.

Drop from a teaspoon onto greased cookie sheets. Bake for 18 minutes, or until the edges of the cookies begin to brown. Cool on wire racks.

PEANUT BUTTER–CHOCOLATE SQUARES

These bear an uncanny resemblance to a well-known candy bar. They freeze well. In fact, some people prefer them frozen.

You can buy graham cracker crumbs or make your own by pulverizing three or four crackers at a time in a food processor.

MAKES 130 1-INCH SQUARES

1 ½ cups graham cracker crumbs (about 15 rectangular crackers)
2 ¾ cups confectioners' sugar
1 cup (2 sticks) margarine, melted
2 cups peanut butter

TOPPING
½ cup (1 stick) margarine
1 12-ounce package semisweet chocolate chips

In a large bowl, combine crumbs and confectioners' sugar and stir. Add melted margarine and peanut butter, and mix well with a wooden spoon. Spread evenly across the bottom of an ungreased 10 × 13-inch jelly roll pan.

To make the topping, melt margarine in a small heavy saucepan. Add chocolate chips, and stir over low heat until completely melted and smooth. Spread evenly over the peanut butter mixture.

Chill, then cut into 1-inch squares.

PEANUT BUTTER–GRANOLA SQUARES

We're not too crazy about raisins. But we can't imagine a snack cookbook that omits them entirely. If your granola has raisins in it already, don't add more. And if your distaste for raisins happens to exceed our own, the recipe works without them.

You won't need an electric mixer for this easy recipe.

MAKES 16 2-INCH SQUARES

⅓ cup margarine
½ cup crunchy peanut butter
¾ cup firmly packed brown sugar
1 egg
1 cup flour
1 teaspoon baking powder
¼ teaspoon salt
2 cups granola
½ cup raisins

Preheat oven to 350°

With a wooden spoon, cream together margarine and peanut butter. Add sugar and egg and stir until well blended.

Stir together flour, baking powder, and salt and add to peanut butter mixture, stirring only until combined. Mix in granola and raisins.

Spread evenly in a lightly greased 8×8-inch baking pan. Bake for 30 minutes, or until lightly browned. Cool thoroughly before cutting into squares.

BREAKFAST AT MIDNIGHT

During exam week at Washington & Lee University,
Breakfast at Midnight is an institution in the school
cafeteria, with professors behind the counters serving up the food. Granted, all the students have to do
is to show up, not make the food. But making it can
be part of the fun. Think about parties and proms,
dancing and skating and midnight dips in lakes or
pools. When they're over, you don't want a wimpy little snack. You want something hearty. And you gen-
erally have at least one co-conspirator to help.

BARBARA MELCHER'S SPICED RICOTTA PANCAKES

Serve these with hot maple syrup or warmed jam.

MAKES ABOUT 20 4-INCH PANCAKES

1 15-ounce container ricotta cheese
5 eggs
1 heaping teaspoon flour
Pinch of salt
1 tablespoon corn oil
½ teaspoon ground cinnamon
¼ teaspoon ground nutmeg

In an electric mixer, beat together ricotta and eggs. Stir in flour, salt, oil, cinnamon, and nutmeg.

Use a quarter-cup measure to ladle the batter onto a hot, lightly greased griddle. When the edges of the pancakes begin to look dry, flip them over and cook on the other side. These take slightly longer to cook than conventional pancakes.

SHARP CHEDDAR CUSTARD

Serve this with Slightly Spicy Tomato Sauce (page 23) or your favorite salsa.

MAKES 4 SERVINGS

Preheat oven to 350°.

Lightly beat *4 eggs* just until the whites and yolks are blended. Then stir in *1½ cups milk, ½ teaspoon salt, freshly ground pepper to taste,* and *¾ cup grated extra-sharp cheddar cheese.* Turn into a greased 9-inch deep-dish pie pan. Set the pie pan inside a larger pan, and pour boiling water into the larger pan until it comes three fourths of the way up the sides of the pie pan. Bake for 25 to 30 minutes, or until the custard is set. Cut into wedges to serve.

WAFFLES FOR TWO

Yes, you can buy frozen waffles and pop them into the toaster in a fraction of the time it takes to make them from scratch. But consider the homemade waffle a snack *activity,* something to do with the family member you bump into in the kitchen at midnight, with the friend who's come to spend the night, or as the romantic conclusion to an evening *à deux.* Here are three variations on the standard waffle, all of which are worth the trouble.

MAKES 2 LARGE WAFFLES

PECAN WAFFLES
½ cup roughly chopped pecans
1 cup sifted flour
1½ teaspoons baking powder
½ teaspoon salt
1 tablespoon sugar
½ teaspoon ground cinnamon
1 egg, separated
¾ cup milk
3 tablespoons corn oil
Butter or margarine, for serving
Pure maple syrup, for serving

Lightly toast pecans in the oven or a toaster oven; set aside to cool.

Combine dry ingredients in a small bowl. In a mug, beat the egg yolk with a fork. Add milk and oil, and stir well. Stir into dry ingredients just long enough to moisten. Add nuts.

In a separate small bowl, beat egg white until stiff. Fold into batter.

Bake in a preheated, lightly oiled waffle iron until done. Serve immediately, with butter and maple syrup if you like.

CHOCOLATE WAFFLES

Omit pecans, sugar, and cinnamon from the first recipe. Add *3 tablespoons chocolate syrup* (and if desired *½ cup chocolate chips*) to batter before folding in egg white. Serve with butter and raspberry syrup. Or with Orange/Cinnamon Butter (page 25). Or go whole hog and serve with vanilla ice cream and Joan's Hot Fudge Sauce (page 25).

CHEESE WAFFLES

Omit pecans, sugar, and cinnamon from the first recipe. Add *¾ cup grated sharp cheddar cheese* before folding in egg white. Serve with Pesto Butter (page 25) or Shallot/Parsley Butter (page 24), or with Slightly Spicy Tomato Sauce (page 23). You may want to add a little milk to the tomato sauce to lighten it up. Or—bit of a surprise— serve these with strawberry or raspberry preserves.

BAKED EGGS ET CETERA

For this recipe you'll need ovenproof ramekins or custard cups that hold about three quarters of a cup. You can make one, or as many as you want.

MAKES 1 SERVING

Preheat oven or toaster oven to 450°.

In the bottom of a greased ovenproof ramekin, place *1 slice of Canadian bacon* and *1 slice of Swiss cheese* (if you want to go to some trouble, you can cut it to fit the cup). Break *2 eggs* into the cup, taking care not to break the yolks. Drizzle *2 to 4 tablespoons milk* over the whites, letting the yolks peek through (leave a little space at the top of the ramekin since the mixture will bubble while cooking). Bake for 8 minutes, sprinkle with *grated Parmesan cheese,* then bake another 8 minutes or until bubbly and golden brown.

BANANA FRENCH TOAST, TWO WAYS

WAY ONE
MAKES 6 SLICES

Break *3 eggs* into a bowl that is wide enough to hold a slice of bread. Add ¼ *cup milk* and *1 teaspoon ground cinnamon* (we like a *lot* of cinnamon), and beat well with a fork. Cut *1 medium banana* into small dice and set aside.

Melt *2 tablespoons margarine* in a large frying pan or griddle, and heat until it sizzles and starts to turn brown. Dip *6 slices of firm white or whole-wheat bread,* one at a time, into batter until well coated on both sides. Shake off excess batter and place the bread in the frying pan. Liberally spoon diced banana over the bread slices. When the bottoms are well browned, flip the slices over and brown the banana-coated sides. Serve with pure maple syrup.

WAY TWO
MAKES 3 SERVINGS

Make French toast as in Way One, but without the diced banana. When the toast is ready, slice *1 or 2 bananas* diagonally to make long oval slices, and mix with just enough *heavy cream* to coat the slices and make them a bit syrupy. Place a piece of French toast on a plate, top with creamy banana slices, and place a second piece of toast on top of that. Serve with pure maple syrup or a fruit syrup.

SLEEPY-TIME BREWS

If that monster in your stomach can be placated with just a drink, there are some wonderful ways to soothe it. And the time involved gives new meaning to the term "instant gratification."

CINNAMON COCOA, THE OLD-FASHIONED WAY

This combination of cinnamon and cocoa has its roots in history: When the Spaniards brought chocolate home from the New World in the sixteenth century, they were apparently unaware that the Aztecs used vanilla to flavor it. For at least two centuries afterwards, they used cinnamon instead of vanilla to flavor both hot chocolate and chocolate confections.

Combine *2 teaspoons Dutch-process cocoa, 1 tablespoon plus 1 teaspoon sugar,* and *¼ teaspoon cinnamon* in a mug. Measure *1 cup milk* and add a little of it to the dry ingredients to make a smooth paste. Add remaining milk, stir well, and heat in the microwave on high for 2½ minutes. (Or, should you be truly old-fashioned, you can make this in a small saucepan over low heat.)

APRICOT YOGURT FRAPPE

MAKES 1 TALL GLASS

Place *⅓ cup canned apricots and their syrup* in a blender with *¾ cup milk* and *2 scoops of vanilla frozen yogurt.* Purée until smooth and frothy.

NOTE: Try this also with canned peaches or pears.

THREE TEAS

MULLED TEA
Prepared mulling spice mixtures are a boon to impatient people who love mulled wine or cider. Try jazzing up a cup of *traditional tea,* such as Earl Grey or English Breakfast, with *2 heaping teaspoons instant mulling spice.*

MAPLE-ALMOND TEA
Brew a cup of *almond-flavored herbal tea* and stir in *1 teaspoon pure maple syrup* (or to taste).

RAOUL'S ORANGE ICED TEA
Go ahead, live a little—make an entire pitcher. You'll be happy to have it around, and you only have to go to the trouble once.

Place *6 tea bags* in a large mixing bowl with the tags hanging over the edge, and carefully pour *8 cups boiling water* over them. Add *sugar to taste,* if desired, and stir well. Then stir in the *juice of 1 orange.* When the tea has steeped and cooled slightly, discard the tea bags, pour into a 2-quart pitcher, and chill.

BANANA MILKSHAKE

When bananas get too ripe, this is a much faster (and actually healthier) way to use them than in the ubiquitous banana bread.

MAKES 1 TALL GLASS

Peel *1 very ripe large banana* and break it into pieces. Place it in a blender along with *¾ to 1 cup lowfat milk* (depending upon the size of the banana) and *½ teaspoon vanilla.* Purée until smooth and frothy.

NOTE: For a berry shake, substitute 1 cup strawberries or raspberries and 3 tablespoons sugar for the banana.

MAPLE FIZZ

If you're a maple aficionado, this is pure amber heaven in a glass.

MAKES 1 TALL GLASS

Add *1 tablespoon maple syrup* to *8 or 9 ounces of seltzer or club soda.* Mix well.

NOTE: If you like a sweeter drink, add 2 tablespoons of syrup. To make a maple soda, add a scoop of vanilla ice cream.

BROWN COW

Brown Cows seem to have gone the way of soda jerks and soda fountains. If you see them at all anymore, they're called Root Beer Floats.

MAKES 1 TALL GLASS

Pour *root beer* over *1 scoop of vanilla ice cream* in a tall glass.

CHILLED FRUIT SHAKE

Whatever you don't drink right away can be refrigerated or frozen.

MAKES 2 8-OUNCE GLASSES

Put about *4 or 5 ice cubes* in a blender. Add *1 sliced fresh peach, 1 cup sliced strawberries, ½ banana, sliced,* and *2 tablespoons each of sugar and water.* Blend on high speed until completely liquefied and frothy.

NOTE: You can experiment with all kinds of substitutions: raspberries for the strawberries (blueberries turn the whole concoction purple), nectarine or—in winter—pineapple or papaya for the peach.

FOOD AS A
WAKE-UP CALL

Abandon every rule, ye who enter here. This chapter

is intended to fuel the all-nighter. It's for anyone

who has developed an intimacy with the wee hours

of the morning: students, campaign workers, execu-

tives. The recipes are designed to keep your little

brain cells alive and kicking. We're talking caffeine

and cholesterol, spices and mega-protein. In defer-

ence to those who may not have access to a proper

kitchen, the recipes are confined to the toaster oven,

the microwave, and the coffeepot. And they're fast.

FOUR-CHEESE SOUP

Naturally the first recipe in this chapter is an exception: It requires a stove. But it *is* fast. It's a great way to use up an assortment of left-over cheeses in the fridge, if you happen to have some; and almost any combination or number of cheeses will work as long as the total weight is about 6 or 7 ounces.

One combination we've tried and liked is 2 ounces fontina, 2 ounces blue cheese, 2 ounces Bel Paese, and ½ cup grated Parmesan. Another is 4 ounces Edam and 2 ounces smoked Gouda.

MAKES 3 CUPS

Melt *3 tablespoons butter or margarine* in a medium-size saucepan and stir in *3 tablespoons flour.* Cook, stirring, over low heat for about 2 minutes. Gradually add *2 cups milk* and *1 bouillon cube,* and whisk or stir over medium heat until the mixture is thickened and smooth. Add *6 or 7 ounces grated or cubed cheese,* and stir constantly with a wooden spoon or whisk until all the cheese is melted and velvety smooth. Serve right away (a skin will form on top if you don't).

NOTE: Blue cheese and Gorgonzola should be crumbled; soft cheeses such as Bel Paese should be cubed; and hard cheese such as Parmesan should be grated. If the combination of cheeses you are using seems bland, add a dash of Tabasco sauce.

CHILI MACARONI AND CHEESE

Unlike anything else in this book, this snack-for-one is wholly reliant upon convenience foods. But we think it's justifiable, given the circumstances for which it is prescribed.

The chili adds a little zip to the bland macaroni and cheese, and the macaroni adds some creaminess. A thick chili is best for this mixture. If you use a thin one, you'll have to drain off some of the liquid; otherwise it will overwhelm the dish. Even convenience foods have their own aesthetic: you don't want to mix the chili and the macaroni too vigorously, or you'll lose the individual flavors that make the mixture interesting.

1 individual frozen macaroni and cheese dinner
1 15-ounce can of your favorite chili
Dash of hot sauce or salsa (optional)

Heat macaroni and cheese in microwave according to package directions. Transfer chili to a microwaveable dish, and heat. Empty macaroni and cheese into a widemouthed bowl, and pour chili on top. Toss together gently. Add hot sauce if you want. (If you feel like gilding the lily, you can add chopped avocado and/or sour cream.)

SPICY MUSHROOM QUESADILLAS

Thanks go to Andrew's friend Michelle Brien, whose recipe we adapted for this book. While traditional quesadillas are usually turnovers that are cut into wedges, we wrapped them so that they could be eaten out of hand. These call for a microwave as well as a toaster oven. They take a little longer than the other recipes in this section—perfect for a procrastinator. If you're in a dorm, invite some friends in to share them, which will delay getting back to work even further.

MAKES 8 QUESADILLAS

½ cup (1 stick) butter or margarine, melted
1 10-ounce package fresh mushrooms, wiped clean and sliced
1 tablespoon dehydrated minced onion
8 8-inch flour tortillas
Grated jalapeño cheddar cheese (or regular cheddar if
  you prefer)

Preheat oven or toaster oven to 400°.

In a 1-quart microwaveable container, combine half the butter with the mushrooms and minced onion. Microwave on high for 3 minutes, or until cooked.

Assemble all the ingredients in a convenient place. One or two at a time, microwave tortillas on high for 30 to 45 seconds, until soft and pliable. Immediately brush lightly with remaining melted butter, fill with 2 tablespoons of the mushroom mixture, and sprinkle with grated cheese. Fold in one side of the tortilla, then roll up from the bottom.

Place the quesadillas seam side down on a foil-covered baking sheet, and brush the tops lightly with some of the remaining melted butter. When all the tortillas have been filled, heat in the oven for a few minutes, until they begin to crisp and brown.

BABY REUBENS

The presence of sauerkraut automatically throws this recipe into the wake-up chapter. It's hard to imagine what kind of dreams you'd have after eating pickled cabbage, if in fact you could fall asleep at all. You'll need a toaster oven to make this.

Take *2 slices of rye bread (not thin-sliced),* and spread one side of each with *soft margarine.* Turn the slices over and spread with *Russian dressing.* Place *a couple of slices of Swiss cheese* and *lean corned beef* on one slice. Top with *several tablespoons of drained sauerkraut* (don't go overboard on the sauerkraut or it will squish out in the toaster oven). Top that with the second slice of bread, margarine side up, and cut diagonally into four diamonds (the "babies"). Place under the broiler until the exposed sides are nicely browned; then turn and brown the other sides.

TEX-MEX DIP

This couldn't be easier, and it's a zingy way to soak up all those corn chips that are lying around.

Preheat oven or toaster oven to 350°.

In a small buttered casserole, mix together *1 16-ounce jar chunky hot salsa; 1 15-ounce can black beans, drained; 2 scallions, sliced; 2 stalks celery, diced; ½ pound Monterey Jack cheese, grated; a handful of chopped fresh cilantro;* and *pepper to taste.* Bake for 15 minutes, or until cheese is melted.

DOUBLE WHAMMY

This is a caffeine overdose in the form of a heady mocha brew. You can add any of the following to either version: heavy cream, whipped cream, marshmallows, vanilla ice cream, or vanilla frozen yogurt.

VERSION ONE
Add *2 tablespoons chocolate syrup* to *1 cup hot coffee.* This version preserves more of the coffee taste and is less sweet, although you could add sugar if you wish.

VERSION TWO
Add *2 heaping tablespoons instant cocoa mix* to *1 cup hot coffee.* This version is sweeter and favors the cocoa taste.